Guid Fasting and Praying: A Way of Fasting And Prayers That Guarantee Results

person to another as such things as faith, persistence, trust, and love for God can determine the outcomes that you receive from the application of the principles in this book.

DEDICATION

This Book is dedicated to the Father, Son, and the Holy Ghost!

TABLE OF CONTENTS

1 Timothy 4:8

For bodily exercise profiteth little: but godliness is profitable unto all things, having promise of the life that now is, and of that which is to come.

CHAPTER ONE

The Necessity of fasting

From the time of old, fasting has been identified with the saints. There were times that the saints of old had to fast because they wanted to hear God or separate themselves from man. This was a discipline that they have to maintain. And we are not different at the present age. We also need fasting to keep our spirit alert to God.

Fasting and prayer is a very potent tool and Jesus had to remind the disciples when they attempted to cast out a devil from a possessed child that this *kind goeth out not, except by prayer and by fasting.* Matthew

7:21   Jesus was simply telling his disciples that they ought to have been fasting before this day and gather fire and not to wait for the trouble before they begin to fast.

The Bible reminds us that Jesus is the same yesterday, today and forever. What he said to his disciples still has a large impact on us today. We have to maintain some level of spiritual discipline with fasting and prayer if we want to see some certain results in life. There are times that we may have to deprive the body of food or water so that our spirit man can be positioned to receive or hear from the Lord. The devil knows that when we begin to fast and pray as the Holy Spirit is leading us, we will be potential ballistic missiles against his kingdom. Once you have the leading to fast, the devil tells you 1000 reasons this fast is not necessary.

But if we must remain potent in our spirituality, we must follow the footsteps of Jesus, and the saints of old who had to fast in order to keep their spirit man spiritually alert to receive from God.

This book was written to guide you on how to make your Christian fasting productive and achieve great spiritual results. I have seen men and women of God in life who fast often and their spiritual exploits are beyond words. I am by no means tying the work of God in their lives to fasting alone. However, I have seen the marvellous things it has done for them.

The more you fast, the greater you empower the spirit inside of you. The lesser you fast, the more you strengthen the flesh, the man outside of you. By extension, if the man outside of you is made bigger, you respond more to the things of the flesh than to the things of the spirit. You become less sensitive to the Spirit of God living inside of you. Divine moments are easily missed because the Holy Spirit is speaking, yet the man can't get what God is saying. Jesus knew this well so he decided to subject his flesh to the life of fasting. Jesus lived a fasted life before the disciples were chosen. He wanted to keep his spirit sensitive in selecting the right people for the discipleship work. He was a man of fasting during the time of his ministry on earth. And we know that the disciples that he chose were the right people because of the exploit that they later made. At one point, the disciples made determined effort to have Jesus eat some food. He refused, telling them that, "I have meat to eat that ye know not of" (John 4:32).

If Jesus had to fast, then we can't exempt ourselves from this way of life. I heard the story of a young man who was encouraged to fast. He told his Christian friends that the anointing he has is not for fasting but for enjoyment. And some believers are like that. They are willing to do everything as long as fasting is kept off their schedules. Soon, a time will come that they must have to fast. When the people met Jesus to ask why the disciples of John the Baptist fast, yet Jesus' disciples don't. He had a profound answer in Mark 2:18-20

18 And the disciples of John and of the Pharisees used to fast: and they come and say unto him, Why do the

disciples of John and of the Pharisees fast, but thy disciples fast not?

19 And Jesus said unto them, Can the children of the bridechamber fast, while the bridegroom is with them? as long as they have the bridegroom with them, they cannot fast.

20 But the days will come, when the bridegroom shall be taken away from them, and then shall they fast in those days.

Jesus was telling his questioners, don't worry. A time is coming that they would fast. And they did fast when Jesus' ministry was completed. Acts 13:2, "they ministered to the Lord and fasted."

As you keep running away from fasting, a time is coming that you will have no option but to fast. That is when some people will set 7 days aside to fast and pray. Their fast would have been more effective if they had been living a fasted life. Setting out a day or two in a week to fast and wait on the Lord. The challenge would have met them ready. The disciples were caught off guard. The demon that traumatized that little boy continued without restraint. Throwing him into the fire and then into the water. They were not ready for that because of the lack of solid fasting life. The best time to prepare for war, as it is often said, is in the time of peace.

Ecclesiastes 10:10

If the iron be blunt, and he do not whet the edge, then must he put to more strength: but wisdom is profitable

CHAPTER TWO

Spiritual Benefits of Fasting

The bible is clear on the spiritual impact of fasting on the believer. 1 Timothy 4:8a *"For bodily exercise profiteth little."* Every spiritual activity that you engage yourself in, there is a spiritual benefit either to your flesh or to your spirit man. When it comes to fasting, the benefits are like a double-edged sword. It has an impact on the flesh and your spirit man. Our generation is full of men and women who look fresh and overweight on the outside, yet the state of the spirit man will fetch a lot of pity from you. It looks thin, malnourished. Why? These people care about tending to their perishable flesh which with time will turn to dust. The spirit of man that abides forever is given little or no attention at all.

The bible says bodily exercise profiteth little. The same is also true concerning spiritual exercise – it profiteth much. The spirit is empowered, sensitivity is increased. In his book, A guide to Fasting, Kenneth .E. Hagin recount how a pastor who never fasted got into a lot of trouble. He kept a constant appointment with food and hardly skips a meal. The outcome is evident in the flesh. He struggled with his flesh a lot and found it difficult to keep his temper down. His wife was constantly the receiver of his fleshly struggle. Whenever you want to do anything that will enhance your spiritual life, the devil will make sustained efforts to ensure that you don't. He will assault you with a thousand reasons why you should not do that activity. I remembered one day when the Holy Spirit had impressed on my heart to do a long fast. When the instruction came for the fast, I began the fast. It was not easy and at some point, I felt like discontinuing the fast. When my fast was gathering days, the devil came, "God wants to kill you. Why does he want you to do this kind of fasting? He does not love you at all."

Praise God that all his determined attacks never succeeded. And I can tell you that what happened to my spiritual life afterword was profound.

Sensitivity

A believer's sensitivity to the Holy Ghost is indispensable to leading a successful Christian life. Albeit this is one area that believers seldom take seriously. God will always speak to you in clear terms what you should do, he won't strife with you. No wonder one of the ways that the Holy Ghost manifest himself is appearing in a bodily manner in the form of a dove (see Luke 3:22). The import of this manifestation is that he is gentle. The dove is a gentle bird.

Matthew 10:16:

> **Behold, I send you forth as sheep in the midst of wolves: be ye therefore wise as**

serpents, and harmless as doves.

He won't struggle with you. He is gentle and that is why sometimes when he wants to communicate with you, he impresses things on your heart. He nudges and not pushes. In the book of Genesis 6:3, one of the main reasons why the generation of Noah was destroyed was because of their striving with the gentle spirit of God. The Holy Spirit that lives in you doesn't struggle. To live in the realm of the Spirit and be in tune with him, you must understand his nature. He is gentle. Most times, his communications are seen in his gentleness. He will impress things on your heart or drop things in your spirit man. Picking them requires a greater level of sensitivity. And that is what fasting does to you. It brings you into a level of sensitivity to receive from the Holy Ghost. The flesh is suppressed, and the spirit is lifted. In Acts 13:2-3, we saw this clearly when the disciples ministered unto the Lord and fasted:

Acts 13:2-3:

2 As they ministered to the Lord, and fasted, the Holy Ghost said, Separate me Barnabas and Saul for the work whereunto I have called them.

3 And when they had fasted and prayed, and laid their hands on them, they sent them away.

The disciples were carrying out a spiritual transaction of fasting and prayer when this word came. They were able to hear what God was saying because the flesh has been subjected to fasting. It became easier for them to hear what the Holy Ghost was saying. Further, they prayed for them and sent them forth. They knew precisely what the Holy Ghost wanted them to do. Unfortunately, so many children of God have missed vital leadings of God in their lives as a result of lack of sensitivity. God spoke or gave a direction that meant a total turn around for their lives but it was missed. They were not sensitive to the leading of the Holy Ghost. It won't have been missed had they subjected their lives to a routine of prayer and fasting.

Service to God

The reason for laxity towards fasting is simply that the believer doesn't look at it beyond food abstinence. Models who stay away from food may be doing so for the purpose of obtaining weight loss. A believers fasting is more than food abstinence. Fasting is a form of service to God. When you are fasting, you are serving God. Fasting and prayer is a form of service to God.

Luke 2:37

And she was a widow of about fourscore and four years, which departed not from the temple, but served God with fastings and prayers night and day.

She served God with fasting and prayers day and night. This was a woman of 84 years who took up the responsibility of praying and fasting. The day believers begin to look at fasting beyond the border of food abstinence, from that moment our fasting life will change. What is the reward of service? Let us look into the scripture to see what happens to those who serve God through fasting and prayer.

Ex 23:25-27

> **25 And ye shall serve the Lord your God, and he shall bless thy bread, and thy water; and I will take sickness away from the midst of thee.**
> **26 There shall nothing cast their young, nor be barren, in thy land: the number of thy days I will fulfil.**
> **27 I will send my fear before thee, and will destroy all the people to whom thou shalt come, and I will make all thine enemies turn their backs unto thee.**

The reward of service is:

- God will bless your bread and water (the works of your hands)

- Healthy life
- Your children shall not die at a young age
- You can't be barren
- Long life

The rewards you get for serving God are listed above. And from the scripture under analysis, we have seen that fasting and prayer is a form of service to the Lord. So we can say that every time you fast and pray, these are the rewards you get. Your fasting is way more than food starvation, it is a form of rendering service to the lord. Those who diligently serve and seek the Lord will be rewarded.

Ability to Cast out Demons

Fasting generates in you the power to cast out demons. The disciples couldn't cast out a demon in Matthew 17:21 due to the dearth of fasting and prayer. Jesus was telling the disciples that you can't cast out this type of demon if you aren't given to the life of fasting.

Matthew 17:21

Howbeit this kind goeth not out but by prayer and fasting.

I know that the authority of the believer is given by the Lord. However, your spiritual fire to cast out demons is enhanced by your fasting and prayer. Practically, it will be impossible to tell the Father of the boy who has seen his son beaten and tormented by the devil to wait another day. We will go and fast and thereafter return back to help your son. The father did not have that time. He was at his wit end. He came to the disciples to help with the situation of his son. He was tired of seeing his son in such a helpless circumstance. Possibly, he might have heard the news that Jesus was around in town and his disciples can do the same work that Jesus was doing. He was confronted with a strong disappointment when his disciples failed in their action to cast the devil that had made life miserable for the poor boy. The boy's father brought him to Jesus. By the way that the devil reacted to the rebuke of Jesus, it is clear that the devil is a stubborn devil.

Mark 9:26-27

26 And the spirit cried, and rent him sore, and came out of him: and he was as one dead; insomuch that many said, He is dead.
27 But Jesus took him by the hand, and lifted him up; and he arose.

The devil didn't want to leave the boy at all. He wanted to continue throwing the boy into the fire and into the water. The devil derived so much pleasure in the sufferings of that boy. The devil shook the boy violently and caused the boy to fall many times before he bade goodbye to his abode, the place where he occupied to work his wickedness.

There is a greater lesson for us to learn from this act of Jesus. Jesus had been living a fasted life. How do we know? He fasted forty days and night. There was a certain time that his disciples persuaded him to eat, yet he refused and told them that he has food to eat which they didn't know about.

John 4:32

> **But he said unto them, I have meat to eat that ye know not of.**

It's obvious he was living a fasted life. He may not have set down that time to fast, but a life of fasting entails that, you may skip meals and food to keep your spirit man active. I have experienced this in my life. Whenever I am full, satisfied with food, connecting to God is often dented with difficulties. I would struggle to connect to God. When I made progress by breaking through the barrier of my flesh, the worship would be hard. Conversely, when I am light, in the mode of fasting and prayer seeking the face of God, my connection to heaven is streamless. I gain entrance to the holy of holies and connect to the Lord.

We know from the scriptures that Jesus lived a fasted life and that was why the devil responded to his rebuke quickly.

Gladly, for the Apostle Paul, he knew this secret very well and confined his life to frequent fasting. He recalled his fasted life thus:

2 Corinthians 11:27

In weariness and painfulness, in watchings often, in hunger and thirst, in fastings often, in cold and nakedness.

I can't be amazed at the level of the miraculous power that he demonstrated. It reached a point where handkerchief from his body was carried to the sick; they were healed.

Strength

Psalms 27:14,

Wait on the Lord: be of good courage, and he shall

strengthen thine heart: wait, I say, on the Lord.

For the Christian, the time of waiting is often combined with prayer and fasting. Where believers dedicate their time to seeking the face of the Lord either for a specific needs or even waiting on him for the purpose of knowing him more.

While many have neglected the place of fasting, it has remained the source of strength. If you want to be strengthened in your Christian walk, then you must embrace the place of fasting. Yet several believers have neglected the biblical injunction to fast and pray. Some people keep their mouths busy as if they have an appointment with food. No wonder if you look at their spiritual lives, it has been earmarked by weakness. They are wondering why they are so spiritually weak, without actually examining their fasting lives. There is a place for strength to be pumped into your life which comes only when you devote yourself to fasting and prayer.

In the book of Psalm, we saw that waiting on God enables him to pour his strength into our hearts. And the heart of man is the throne of God. Every believer you see who is fervently serving the Lord, check the state of his heart and you will see that the heart is fortified.

Even the Gospel of Jesus Christ begins from the heart. A drop of the word into your heart begins a great transformation that changes an entire nation.

Renewal of Strength

Isaiah 40:31

> *But they that wait upon the Lord shall renew their strength; they shall mount up with wings as eagles; they shall run, and not be weary; and they shall walk, and not faint.*

Quoting scriptures is good but what releases the power of the word of God into our lives isn't how much we quote the scripture! It lies in how much we do the scriptures.

Isaiah 40:31 is one of the frequently quoted scriptures yet how many times do we leave the realm of quoting into the realm of doing.

This may be my personal opinion, but it is substantially true in a different respect. A car travelling on the interstate road may need to stop several times to feed its tank with gasoline. If the car continues the journey and ignores the warning signals frequently flashing on the dashboard for gasoline, that car will stop its journey due to the lack of gas. This same analogy is true for our spirit man.

You have been doing enormous things for the Lord and bless God for that. You may not feel tired physically but spiritually you may be tired. You can only renew your strength in the place of fasting and prayer where you wait on the Lord. Interestingly, some of the greatest spiritual problems that confront our lives can be solved by moments of waiting. Where strength is renewed, and we are fired up to continue the race doing the work of the Lord fervently.

In the circular world, some of these principles are applied. The soccer team often calls a time out. A half time period of 15 minutes where the coaches tell the players new strategies to use to sustain their winning. If, on the other hand, they are losing a new strategy to use in order to draw upon level points and win. They will rest for 15 minutes. In basketball, timeouts are frequently called. Whatever sporting activity you think of there are moments given to the teams to strategize.

You may not call a timeout spiritually but each time you wait on the Lord, it is like a spiritual timeout where you spend time with the Lord for your strength to be renewed.

Every believer who desires a renewal of strength must never neglect the path of fasting and prayer. To avoid weariness in your walk with the Lord, then wait on the Lord in fasting from time to time.

The Voice of God

Acts 13:2

As they ministered to the Lord, and fasted, the Holy Ghost said, Separate me Barnabas and Saul for the work whereunto I have called them.

The place of fasting and prayer is the place for hearing the voice of God. When you engage yourself in fasting and prayers, especially when you combine such fasting with intense worship and praise, it is very easy to hear the voice of God.

It is an error for a believer to relegate the place of fasting and prayer in his life to a hunger strike. A spiritual exercise of fasting and prayer is beyond food abstinence. Its benefits include opening your spirit man to hear the voice of the Lord. It was when the disciples ministered to the Lord and fasted that they heard God's voice directing them to set aside Saul and Barnabas for a special mission. If you read the book of Acts further down, you will see that after they prayed for them and set them apart, the two went ahead to achieve great things for the Lord together.

Imagine that the disciples were not fasting but rather committed themselves to eat all the time. They would have missed the voice of God. This would have impacted the kingdom of God greatly because Paul and Barnabas are supposed to do great work for God.

There was a time in scripture that the disciples were hedged by the problem of food among the believers. Since food wasn't their primary concern, they responded nicely in Acts 6:2:

Then the twelve called the multitude of the disciples unto them, and said, It is not reason that we should leave the word of God, and serve tables.

Keeping a constant life of fasting and prayer opens you for the voice of the Lord.

Destroying Bondage

Isaiah 58:6-7

> *Is not this the fast that I have chosen? to loose the bands of wickedness, to undo the heavy burdens, and to let the oppressed go free, and that ye break every yoke?*

The believer's life isn't free from satanic attacks! Truly, there are some believers living in bondage! It is not the will of God. He has given us all the authority to break the bondage of our lives. When I speak about bondage, it isn't limited only to demonic oppression. A man can be living in financial bondage, health bondage, etc. A woman can also be living in marital bondage. Even though the man may be the perfect will of God for her, the enemy keeps the family under his watch. Attacking the family with bouts of strife. Turning the husband against the wife.

Believers can be living in financial bondage! It is the perfect will of God for them to be blessed, yet they are struggling financially.

Psalms 35:27

Let them shout for joy, and be glad, that favour my righteous cause: yea, let them say continually, Let the Lord be magnified, which hath pleasure in the prosperity of his servant

You don't need to sit down whining! Take up your mantle and declare a time of fasting and prayers! If you can do that, you can easily break the yoke of the devil off your family or off your life. Fasting and prayer is a powerful weapon for breaking yokes and destroying bondages.

Thwarting the Enemy's plan

I will be very careful with this subtopic so that I am not misunderstood. We aren't supposed to live in fear of the plan of the devil against our lives. Yet it is our prayers and fasting that destroys the plans of the devil.

In America, we recently saw the rise of certain sins which the bible forbids!

Homosexuality was legalized. A Christian woman by the name Kim Davies refused to register and subsequently issue a license to gay couples in 2016. She was jailed for standing for her faith. However, she was released five days later. The handwriting on the American wall that it was heading into this deep, dark funnel of sin is everywhere. What's the responsibility of you and me? God expects us to pray for our nations.

If fasting and prayer had been taken up seriously, this wouldn't have happened. Fasting and prayer would have been used to destroy the plans of the devil to throw America into this sin.

Esther 4:16-17

16 Go, gather together all the Jews that are present in Shushan, and fast ye for me, and neither eat nor drink three days, night or day: I also and my maidens will fast likewise; and so will I go in unto the king, which is not

according to the law: and if I perish, I perish.
17 So Mordecai went his way, and did according to all that Esther had commanded him.

It was the prayer and fasting of Esther, Mordecai and the people of the Jews that saved them from total annihilation. The devil had perfectly planned their destruction, but it was only fasting and prayers that saved them and prevented the enemy from having his way.

Obtaining Favour

You need a favour, then learn to subject yourself to a life of prayer and fasting. Some things that you are asking God for may be in the hands of men. You can go before God and ask him for it so that you may obtain favour from the Lord.

Proverbs 21:1

The king's heart is in the hand of the Lord, as the rivers of water: he turneth it whithersoever he will.

One of the beloved sisters I knew shared this wonderful testimony with me. Jessica was fervent and lived a fasted life while in school. She had other siblings. Each semester as it is customary in Nigeria, this part of the world where I live, parents often give students pocket money. This is the money that you will have in your pocket for sundry expenses. Jessica and her brother were both schooling in the Benue State University, the College where I graduated from. Before she asked her father anything, she would spend the night praying. Then the next morning she would ask her dad what she wanted for school, and her father will give her all that she asked for. Her brother was surprised and would complain about why their father gives everything that Jessica ask for. Jessica would laugh.

I wasn't surprised by her testimony. If you want to go for a job interview, a business proposal conference, a presentation in school, subject yourself to a time of prayer and fasting. If you gain favour from the creator of men, then it won't be difficult to find favour with men.

Some people wonder why they had the best idea yet they were rejected. They simply didn't get favour from God. There are people who made sacrifices to different altars before going for job interviews. Others make incantations before doing a business presentation. However, the believer is contended to go there empty without fasting and praying to obtain favour. You may have the best idea, but it will be rejected because you have failed to pray and fast and obtain favour from the men you are supposed to make a presentation before.

When Esther wanted to go before the King, she fasted. When Nehemiah wanted to go before the King, he fasted! Both of them got what they asked for!

Yet we don't want to. It is only results that we want! The day we give fasting and prayer its rightful place in our lives, that day our whole life will change.

Fasted Life

We have cited several scriptures above that made it clear for us that the best life to live is fasted life. It means fasting becomes your way of life. You may not be fasting on a particular day, but the desire to eat may not be there. You may skip a meal or two due to the need to fast. When fasting becomes your way of life, you are loading your spiritual man with power that will make every demon bow to the authority in the name of Jesus. Another example of someone who had lived a fasted life in scripture is Anna. She was aged and had gathered great days in her earthly life. She served God with prayer and fasting. She lived a fasted life. Fasting and prayer became identified with her way of life (Luke 2:37-38)

Divine Activity

Fasting and prayer can provoke divine activity. As you fast and pray, it is possible to cause a spiritual movement to occur.

Acts 10:30-31

> *30 And Cornelius said, Four days ago I was fasting until this hour; and at the ninth hour I prayed in my house,*

and, behold, a man stood before me in bright clothing,
31 And said, Cornelius, thy prayer is heard, and thine alms are had in remembrance in the sight of God.

This man was a great giver. He had been giving for a long time. Notice what the angel said to him, Cornelius, your alms have been acknowledged by God. He was giving and kept giving. Nothing happened until the day that he decided to pray and fast. At the moment of fasting and prayer, a divine activity happened. His prayer and fasting provoked the release of an angel from heaven.

Acts 10:19-20

19 While Peter thought on the vision, the Spirit said unto him, Behold, three men seek thee.
20 Arise therefore, and get thee down, and go with them, doubting nothing: for I have sent them.

The fasting and prayer of this man even caused the Holy Ghost to speak to Peter. His fasting and prayer caused a divine activity to happen. An angel appeared to him, and the Holy Ghost spoke to Peter. Plus, his family was saved and they were baptised with the Holy Ghost and began to pray in tongues. The fasting and prayer of one man have caused a chain reaction. Plus, many people that were present on the day that Peter preached, were saved.

Acts 10:46, 48

> **46 For they heard them speak with tongues, and magnify God. Then answered Peter,**
> **48 And he commanded them to be baptized in the name of the Lord. Then prayed they him to tarry certain days.**

Discipline

Nothing keeps the body under check and discipline like fasting. The Psalmist understood this fact that was why he brought his body under the regime of fasting. The flesh if allowed on its own may want what will ordinarily destroy the spirit. Your fasting helps your body to co-operate with the spirit.

Great Results

Certain results in your life can be achieved when you accept the life of prayer and fasting. Nehemiah was serving as a cupbearer in a foreign land when Hanani visited Nehemiah and informed him of the status of things in Jerusalem how the gates of Jerusalem were broken, and the scenes were that of great affliction. He was so troubled and he knew that to achieve anything, he needed great favour from the King. He needed to ask the king under whose reign they were in captivity for the favour of returning back to Jerusalem to build its broken walls.

He spent his time in prayers and fasting.

Nehemiah 1:2-5

2 That Hanani, one of my brethren, came, he and certain men of Judah; and I

35

asked them concerning the Jews that had escaped, which were left of the captivity, and concerning Jerusalem.

3 And they said unto me, The remnant that are left of the captivity there in the province are in great affliction and reproach: the wall of Jerusalem also is broken down, and the gates thereof are burned with fire.

4 And it came to pass, when I heard these words, that I sat down and wept, and mourned certain days, and fasted, and prayed before the God of heaven,

When he committed himself to fast and to pray before the Lord, he sought the favour from the King and his request was granted for him to go and build the walls of Jerusalem. The king saw that his face appeared disfigured by distress. The king asked him what he wanted. He had already fasted and obtained favour from the Lord so it was not difficult to get it from the hand of a man. God has the heart of the Kings in his hands and he turns it in whatever direction that he desires. There are some of us who are looking for a favour from their supervisor or boss at their job. You have done it in the flesh for a long time. It is time to change your approach. Obtain favour from the Lord. Take it to the Lord in prayer and fasting and see what happens. A man who knows how to fast and pray is a man that will get any result that he desires.

Power

If you need power, then you should commit yourself to a life of fasting and prayer. Throughout scripture, we saw how men and women who served the Lord walked in dynamic power as a result of the life of fasting. During his earthly ministry on earth, Jesus committed himself to fasting and prayer.

Luke 4:1-2

And Jesus being full of the Holy Ghost returned from

Jordan, and was led by the Spirit into the wilderness,
2 Being forty days tempted of the devil. And in those days he did eat nothing: and when they were ended, he afterward hungered.

After Jesus had fasted, in verse 14, the Bible tells us the outcome of that spiritual exercise.

And Jesus returned in the power of the Spirit into Galilee: and there went out a fame of him through all the region round about.

When the fasting was over, Jesus returned in the power of the Spirit. He began to teach and preach. His ministry, after this spiritual fast opened. If you read further, you will see the result of the power of the Spirit that came into his life. His ministry took a different dimension. We have considered Matthew 17:21 when Jesus told the disciples that this kind can't be cast out except by prayer and fasting. Through the death of

Jesus, we have been given authority over the power of darkness. Mark 16:17, we would see that all those who believe in Jesus have been given authority over the works of darkness. Don't confuse power and authority. You can have the authority, but the power to enforce the authority may be lacking completely.

There was a time that I took a long fast. In the fourth day of my fast, that evening when the moon hung tightly on the sky, I stepped out to pray that night. I went to the Basketball Court of the Benue State University, Makurdi, Benue State, Nigeria to pray that evening. I prayed for a while before one of the fervent sisters in the Campus, Ene, came out to pray that night. She was so prayerful that she was named Ene-Prayer. She met me, and we prayed and joined our faith together according to the word of the Lord in Mathew 18:19. That night, she went back to the dormitory, and her appetite for food died. She ate nothing that evening. The next day, the same thing continued. She felt strange and forced herself to eat that evening. Immediately, she felt that the Holy Ghost convicted her about the food she ate. I believe power jumped into her that day and the desire for food died.

One of the greatest benefits of fasting and prayer to the believer is that it generates so much power. If you want the power to be available in your life, then plug yourself to the switch of fasting and prayer. We can see this in scripture when Jesus fasted and prayed, he returned back in power. So we know from scripture that when you fast and pray, you plug yourself into the socket of power. If you are in need of spiritual power, the first thing you should do is to cultivate the life of fasting and prayer. It is in the place of fasting and prayer that power is made available. This is the kind of lifestyle Jesus led while he was on earth. If we are truly his disciples, then we will not abandon the place of fasting and prayer in our lives.

If a believer lives his life as if he has a covenant with food, that believer will be a powerless believer. The absence of the life of fasting and prayer is the dearth of spiritual power. You want to see power, then embrace the life of fasting and prayer.

We saw in the book of Luke chapter 4 how Jesus was led to fast, he followed the leading of the Holy Spirit. There are times that the Holy Spirit will lead you to pray and fast. That has to do with leading. But at other times, you can decide to mark certain days of the week for fasting and prayer.

We saw the outcome of Jesus fasting and prayer in Luke 4:14. He came back in the power of the spirit of God and the Bible says that his fame spread abroad. There is something fasting can do for you if you can plug yourself into the power of prayer and fasting. Neglect of the place of prayer and fasting is to completely ignore the power of God that can only be obtained through fasting.

The life of fasting and prayer is something that you must give serious consideration to. The impact of fasting and prayer will affect every sphere of your Christian life. When Jesus began to preach after he fasted, he enjoyed remarkable power to the extent that the people who were listening to him started to confess and marvel that his words came with so much power?

Luke 4:31-32

> **31 And came down to Capernaum, a city of Galilee, and taught them on the sabbath days.**
> **32 And they were astonished at his doctrine: for his word was with power.**

Jesus' example is what we are supposed to imbibe. He lived a fasted life. He knew the kind of power that fasting and prayer generated in his life, so he was committed to this way of living. Conversely, the disciples of Jesus preferred the joy of eating than fasting.

Luke 5:33-35

> **33 And they said unto him, Why do the disciples of John fast often, and make prayers, and likewise the disciples of**

the Pharisees; but thine eat and drink?

34 And he said unto them, Can ye make the children of the bridechamber fast, while the bridegroom is with them?

35 But the days will come, when the bridegroom shall be taken away from them, and then shall they fast in those days

Jesus told them, hey, don't worry they will fast. It is just a matter of time. But Jesus led a life of fasting. The disciples begged him, "Sir, would you please have some quick meal?"

Jesus responded in John 4:31-32

31 In the mean while his disciples prayed him, saying, Master, eat.

32 But he said unto them, I have meat to eat that ye know not of.

If you are not used to fasting and praying, begin now and the difference in your life will be very clear.

Deliverance from Temptation

Fasting and prayer can deliver you from temptation. This is what Jesus was trying to explain to his disciples that if they failed to watch and pray, they would fall into temptation. In that book of the Bible, what Jesus told his disciples was to watch and then pray. So we can say that praying will deliver you from temptation. *"Fasting and prayer."*

That is what you are doing. When you fast and pray, you are performing an important exercise that will keep you from falling into temptation.

Matthew 26:37-41

> *And he took with him Peter and the two sons of Zebedee, and began to be sorrowful and very heavy.*
> *38 Then saith he unto them, My soul is exceeding*

44

sorrowful, even unto death: tarry ye here, and watch with me.

39 And he went a little further, and fell on his face, and prayed, saying, O my Father, if it be possible, let this cup pass from me: nevertheless not as I will, but as thou wilt.

40 And he cometh unto the disciples, and findeth them asleep, and saith unto Peter, What, could ye not watch with me one hour?

41 Watch and pray, that ye enter not into temptation: the spirit indeed is willing, but the flesh is weak.

When you are fasting and praying, you are safeguarding yourself against temptation. When Jesus told the disciples to watch and pray, and they didn't heed to his counsel, did they fall into temptation? Yes, they did. Let me show you.

Matthew 26:51

And, behold, one of them which were with Jesus stretched out his hand, and drew his sword, and struck a servant of the high priest's, and smote off his ear.

John 18:10

Then Simon Peter having a sword drew it, and smote the high priest's servant, and cut off his right ear. The servant's name was Malchus.

Uncle Peter who should have prayed himself out of this temptation of using violence against another person refused and fell into temptation and sin. He used his sword and cut off the ear of another man because of Jesus. This is exactly what Jesus was telling him. Watch and pray.

When you fast, you not only stay away from food alone. It is a defence against temptation. You are engaging yourself in one of the spiritual exercises that deliver from temptation. The lesser you fast and pray, the more predisposed you will be to temptation.

I believe strongly that if Peter had prayed, he would have escaped that temptation of acting violently towards **Malchus.** The bible didn't tell us, but I believe it was the mercies of God that saved Peter if not, he would have been arrested for injuring another. Jesus healed the man instantly and told Peter:

> *Then said Jesus unto him, Put up again thy sword into his place: for all they that take the sword shall perish with the sword.*

(Matthew 26:52)

Peter was rebuked by Jesus. Meaning that, if only you had watched and prayed with me, you won't have acted the way you did. I told you repeatedly to watch and pray, yet you refused to listen. Now, can you see the repercussion of your prayerlessness?

Your prayer and fasting will deliver you from falling into temptation. Show me a believer who doesn't embrace the life of fasting and prayer, and I will tell you that this believer can easily fall prey to temptation. This is what the bible says.

It doesn't matter where you are today. You can begin to fast and pray, and your prayer will shift your spiritual life. If you want to escape the snare that the devil will cast on your path, begin now by learning the life of fasting and prayers.

Peters fall into sin and iniquity did not stop after the encounter in the garden. He continued into more sin. Peter was beating his chest that he will go anywhere Jesus goes but was the first to later deny Jesus. He said even if all men will fall apart from you, I will be with you. But a prayerless man can make promises that he will never be able to keep.

Luke 22:33

And he said unto him, Lord, I am ready to go with thee, both into prison, and to death.

As far as promises are concerned, Peter has no words to spare. He freely spoke about how he can die and be crucified with Jesus Christ. Was he able to keep his promises? Well, the subsequent Scripture will tell us.

Luke 22:56-60

56 But a certain maid beheld him as he sat by the fire, and earnestly looked upon him, and said, This man was also with him.

57 And he denied him, saying, Woman, I know him not.

58 And after a little while another saw him, and said, Thou art also of them. And Peter said, Man, I am not.

59 And about the space of one hour after another confidently affirmed, saying, Of a truth this fellow also was with him: for he is a Galilaean.

60 And Peter said, Man, I know not what thou sayest. And immediately, while he yet spake, the cock crew.

It was the same Peter that was lifting up his voice to heaven telling Jesus that he will go anywhere with him. Yet this same man was so fearful that he denied Jesus three times. Not only did he do that, even before a little girl he said he never knew Jesus. Brethren, they more prayerless you become, the easier it is for you to fall into sin and to temptation. If Peter had prayed in the garden as Jesus had told them to, I believe that he wouldn't have fallen into sin the way he did. He was fearful, that he denied Jesus even before a maid. Other translations of the Bible will tell you that Peter denied Jesus before a little girl. One of the greatest things prayer and fasting does to you is that it imparts you with the nature and the character of God. As you draw near to God in prayer as a result of your fasting, you come in contact with the presence of God and the presence of God releases upon you the nature and the character of God which is fearlessness and boldness. Have you ever seen a scripture where it said God was fearful? If he wasn't, then you can't. That is what would have happened to Peter if he had prayed in the garden as he was directed by Jesus to do.

Matthew 17:21

Howbeit this kind goeth not out but by prayer and fasting.

CHAPTER THREE

The Scientific Benefit of Fasting and Prayer

Interestingly, the benefits of fasting are not limited to your spiritual life alone. At least, scientists have something to say about how fasting affects your life and promotes the general wellbeing of the body and by extension, your health. There are some illnesses today that don't need any medication, they require a life of discipline. Now, before I am quoted wrong, I am not discouraging the use of drugs. In fact, medicine is a gift from God; and we owed praises to God for all our Christian doctors around the world. The giant strides in the field of medicine are tremendous and praise God for that.

Yet when it comes to issues of overweight, sometimes, the problem lies with the inability to control food cravings. Overweight can be caused by a medical problem too. In that case, a doctor may need to check you and tell you what you need to do.

Let me state it clearly as I did in the topic the necessity of fasting and prayer, what the bible says about the scientific benefits of fasting. We will find this in the book of Timothy.

Timothy 4:8a *"For bodily exercise profiteth little"*

When you fast, it is a bodily exercise because your flesh is being subjected to a form of exercise – self-control from eating food. From scripture, we can see that your body profits little from it. When God speaks about something being small, to the man, it can be enormous. What is a hard thing to do in our sight, is but a light thing in the eyes of the

Lord. I want us to consider the little profit of fasting to the body as captured in the bible from the mind of the scientist.

Body Ketones

Under normal dietary circumstances, the body thrives on carbohydrate, carbs for short. That is the regular source of energy that the body lives and survives on. When you engage yourself in fasting and prayer, especially long fast, your body is sustained by the remaining stock of carbs left in your body. As you continue praying and fasting, your carb store becomes used up. At this juncture, there is nothing more for your body to live on. Your body begins to source for alternative energy to live on. Fat stored in various parts of the body are broken down to service the energy need of the human body. The breaking down of these fat stores in the body leads to ketosis. Ketones are produced during the process of ketosis. Your brain and other vital organs need ketones to work. They are supplied with the right type of energy for effective functioning.

As these fat stores are used steadily by the body system, you lose weight physically. While some people made the pursuit of weight loss their single goal, which I am not against what you do to live healthily, you can get this benefit through prayer and fasting. Your spirit man is empowered to be sensitive to the Holy Spirit and your physical body also benefits.

Body Detoxifier

We are still considering the bodily exercise that profits little. Your fasting and prayer is a body cleanser. It cleanses your body from toxins that might have accumulated over the years. Fasting and prayer is a great detoxifying tool. The vital organs of the body such as the liver, the kidney, the heart all make use of ketones. Your accumulated fat in your body system is used by the body to store toxins. If the toxins are not stored in your body system, it could harm and jeopardize your health. When your fasting and prayer proceeds further, your normal carb stores are used up and fat becomes the only source of energy that your body relies on. When your body enters ketosis, ketones are build up in your body. The fat stored with toxins in your body is broken and important organs of the body use it. The kidney and other organs of the body eliminate these toxins out of the body. This is what the bible said that it profits your body little. If this is a little profit, then I think it is a great one.

Proverbs 1:20

Wisdom crieth without; she uttereth her voice in the streets:

CHAPTER FOUR

Types of Fasting

For the present day believer whose life is regulated by the guidance and the leadership of the Holy Spirit, and who doesn't walk under the law but under grace, the believer is required to obey the instructions of the Holy Spirit as long as those instructions do not contradict the truth of the word of God. He is mandated to obey what God tells him through the Holy Spirit. Under the new covenant, God has codified his laws in our spirit by the Holy Ghost. If what the Holy Spirit told the believer is according to scriptural truth, it follows that the child of God should fast according to the instructions of the Holy Spirit.

You may come home hungry and tired and have imagined what meal you want to have for dinner, but the moment you turned opened the Kitchen door, the Holy Spirit said to skip this dinner or lunch. It becomes law for you at the moment. While the old covenant was administered by the blood of bulls and goats, the new covenant is administered by Jesus through the Holy Spirit. Our spiritual lives will skyrocket in growth when we are able to cooperate with the Spirit of all Spirit, the Holy Ghost. Your fast becomes effective when you follow his leading. The Holy Spirit may tell you to eat one meal a day or tells you to eat only in the morning. He may also tell you to eat only in the evening. If you have heard something like this, your obligation as a child of God is to carry out the direction of the Holy Ghost because they do not violate scriptural truths.

Your fasting should also come under the leading and the guidance of the Holy Spirit. Knowing that the believers are led by God, I don't want to lay down rules and regulation for fasting. The Bible encourages us to fast but didn't say in what manner the fast is to be carried out. This is essential when it comes to fasting. You should be flexible in your fast and allow for the leading of the Holy Ghost.

Listen to the instruction that the Holy Spirit gives you. When Jesus was on earth, we saw a profound lesson when Mary commanded the people at the wedding in Canaan of Galilee, *"His mother saith unto the servants, Whatsoever he saith unto you, do it."* (John 2:5). That should be our attitude towards the Holy Spirit, the administrator of the new covenant.

Interestingly the believers of old fasted under an old covenant, yet they saw so many results from their fast.

Fasting achieves greater results when you allow the Holy Spirit to lead and guide you in your fast because the bible says in the book of Romans 8:2:

For the law of the Spirit of life in Christ Jesus hath made me free from the law of sin and death.

There is a law and we operate under it. The beauty of this law is that the Holy Ghost is the one who guides us lovingly to obey it. If the Holy Spirit tells you to fast in any manner, do it that way. I was fasting one day and I worked so hard doing house chores.

When I finished, I heard the Holy Ghost said, "break this fast now."

I responded reluctantly, "Yes, Lord."

I didn't want to. But that will amount to disobeying the Holy Spirit.

When I had broken the fast, "you are the reason why this fast was broken. Next time, when you want to fast, you should avoid doing excessive work."

I believe that the Holy Ghost saw how overbearing this would be for my body. I simply obeyed and ended my fast prematurely. The lesson here is clear, he is the one that guides and directs. I wrote this to make you understand that under the New Covenant, it is what the Holy Ghost says that stand as the law. Be flexible when fasting and always listening to the nudging of that still small voice of the Holy Ghost.

I will make an effort in categorising the type of fast which a believer can do and support them with scriptures. Plus, never fast to impress anybody. You're not also to fast to make a point. Don't copy another person's style of fasting because you may not know the instructions that he had received from the Holy Ghost. Never attempt to fast because you have heard that somebody fasted for a very long time. Fasting and prayer is a service to God, you should do it believing and trusting the Lord that he will reward and bless you for the fasting and prayer. If the motive of the fast is wrong, the blessings will be missed. God weighs the motive of your fast.

Proverbs 16:2

All a man's ways seem innocent to him, but motives are weighed by the Lord

(NIV)

We will draw lessons from scriptural truth and the Patriarchs of old as to the type of fasting that we can do.

Dry fast

This type of fast is common in scripture among the Jewish who fasted without drinking water or eating any type of food for days. One very striking feature of this fast is that it was carried out in old times for the purpose of repentance or coming before the Lord to obtain favour. The people would mourn and fast before the Lord until they are forgiven from their sins.

Jonah 3:7-10

7 And he caused it to be proclaimed and published through Nineveh by the decree of the king and his nobles, saying, Let neither man nor beast, herd nor flock, taste any thing: let them not feed, nor drink water:

8 But let man and beast be covered with sackcloth, and cry mightily unto God: yea, let them turn every one from his evil way, and from the violence that is in their hands.

9 Who can tell if God will turn and repent, and turn away from his fierce anger, that we perish not?

10 And God saw their works, that they turned from their evil way; and God repented of the evil, that he had said that he would do unto them; and he did it not.

When the people of Nineveh needed forgiveness from the Lord, they fasted without food or water. No one ate food nor drank water.

The fasting of the Jewish was not restricted to repentance alone but extended to obtaining favour from the Lord.

Esther 4:16

Go, gather together all the Jews that are present in Shushan, and fast ye for me, and neither eat nor drink three days, night or day: I also and my maidens will fast likewise; and so will I go in unto the king, which is not according to the law: and if I perish, I perish.

Here, we saw when the plan of the wicked enemy of the Jews was trying to eliminate all of them. Esther had to gather all the people of the Jews to fast and pray. What they did in this circumstance was a dry fast. The bible says they did not eat nor drink for three days. She ate no food or water when they fasted. Esther was fasting so that she can obtain favour from the Lord who has the heart of Kings in his hands.

This is of type of fast, however, it is to be carried out with caution. You should only do a long fast if the Holy Spirit is leading you to do it. If you are pregnant or a breastfeeding mum do not attempt this kind of fast because your baby will need food and when you are lactating you need to feed your baby. As a pregnant or breastfeeding mom, you should consider another type of fasting that we would discuss. I suggest that you carry out this type of fasting when you are led. Where the Holy Spirit leads, he supplies the strength to fast. The bible says it's not by might nor by power, but by the Spirit says the Lord.

Water fast

With this type of fasting, you take only water. No solid food is consumed when this fast is being undertaken. Again, be led by the Holy Spirit before you do any fast that can have a massive impact on your body.

Daniel 1:12

Prove thy servants, I beseech thee, ten days; and let them

give us pulse to eat, and water to drink.

Daniel refused to partake of the king's table because he had proposed in his heart he won't eat anything that would defile his body. The bible did not say that they fasted, but eating only vegetable and water only is a type of fast. Let's look at that scripture very critically. You will see that it is joined by a conjunction vegetable and water to drink. So we can say that it's possible for them to eat vegetables for ten days or decided to take only water. Water fasting is a type of fast that you can do. By drinking water alone, your body stays hydrated during the period of your fast.

Any fasting that will impact your body or a long fast must be under the leading of the Holy Spirit. If you are under the leadership or guidance of a pastor, seek his counsel. Don't fast in this manner if the Holy Spirit isn't leading you to. Fasting takes a lot of energy and strength is needed to perform basic activities in the course of your day.

We saw from scripture that Daniel and his friends combined the two types of fast – water and vegetables. It is possible that they could have fasted on vegetables or water but they combined the two.

Fruits or vegetable

We have looked it at in Daniel 1:12. You restrain yourself from eating all other types of food except vegetables. This isn't a vegan lifestyle but a spiritual activity that you do to heighten your sensitivity to God. Drink water too when undertaking this type of fasting.

How to prepare your body for fasting

Preparing your body before you begin your fast is essential to a productive fast. Have you ever seen believers who are fasting and can't walk for a little distance? They look weak, their faces look disfigured. You had so much pity on them as if you should tell them to stop the fasting.

This is not far-fetched from the fact that they were not prepared for the fast in the first place. Fasting is a spiritual activity, but it's also a physical activity and because it's physical and we still live in the flesh, it requires a lot of strength and energy from us. It's necessary for you to prepare your body for the activity you are about to start. If you are fasting for the first time or you haven't done a long fast for some times, it will be wrong to proceed into a long fast without giving your body the needed time to adjust to the changes. When that is done, the overbearing consequences of the fast on your body will be too much. Prepare yourself and take it one step at a time until your body adapts to the new spiritual activity.

Start fasting until 12 pm or take a shorter fast. The next day, fast until 6 pm. Subsequently, stretch your fast to 8 p.m. and observe. You can begin to prepare for a longer fast. However, if you decide to start fasting for a long period, you can break down and it becomes a problem. Never start a long fast when you have never tried it. A shorter fast is important before embarking on a long fast.

You should also start your fast by making demands for the help of God so that he pours his power and strength on you. The bible says by strength shall no man prevail.

Basic Fasting Etiquette

What to do when you're doing a long fast. It doesn't matter whether you are doing a water fast or vegetable fast, there are basic things that you are required to do. You must always brush your teeth because you are not eating. Your mouth may be smelling if you're not careful. Brush your teeth all the time so you can constantly have fresh breath. Ensure that you brush your tongue very well so that it doesn't smell because most of the smell that comes out from the mouth is as a result of the dirt on the tongue.

Regular shower all the time when you are carrying out a long fast is essential to enable you to stay hydrated because the pores on your skin absorb liquid. That accounts for the reason why when you're carrying out a long fast and you go to the bathroom to get a shower, you feel energized because your body absorbs water.

Brushing Your Teeth All the Time

If you have ever fasted for a long period of time, you would understand what I mean. Your mouth tends to be dry. As a result of that, you will notice that you have bad breath. For most people, this kind of feeling is not convenient. And it can easily interrupt the fasting schedule. They tend to be put off because of the bad breath that comes from their mouth and becomes very discouraged to fast because of the smell.

This is a normal occurrence for believers who fast often. Bad breath in the mouth often occurs when the mouth is dry. When you are fasting and you are not eating food, especially prolong fast your mouth emits a very bad smell. This is caused by dryness in the mouth.

Bad breath in the mouth during periods of fasting is caused by dryness in the mouth. Due to the lack of adequate liquid in the mouth, bacteria in the mouth are not easily flushed out. That is the reason why you should always wash your mouth with water when you are fasting for a long period.

The common occurrence of bad breath is known in the scientific world as halitosis. The chief causes of halitosis are:

1. Food particles in the mouth.
2. Dryness in the mouth
3. Dental diseases.

If the problem of your bad breath is number three above, then you may need to see a doctor before carrying out a long fast. This is necessary so that the doctor will tell you what to do to avoid bad breath

We need to employ wisdom when fasting for a long period. We must not allow dryness in the mouth to put off people from talking to us because of the bad breath. You will notice if you have a bad smell in the mouth, each time you talk to people they would try to keep a reasonable distance from your face. This shows that they're put off by the smell that is coming from your mouth.

There is a way of dealing with bad breath from the mouth during fasting. You have to learn to take care of your mouth before you engage in any type of long fast. Each time you eat food, particles of what you eat is deposited on your tongue. This is the cause of bad breath during the long fast.

The best way to deal with the bad smell before you start the fast is to scrape your tongue. You can buy any tongue scraper from any available store near you. With that, you can place the tongue scraper at the back of your tongue and scrape every particle on your tongue that causes bad breath.

Each time dryness in the mouth is avoided when fasting, the root cause of bad breath has been taken care of. To this effect, you may rinse your mouth with water several times in a day to do away with bad breath. As a personal principle, whenever I engage in long fast I make sure that my mouth is well hydrated. Sometimes I brush my mouth very well several times in the day. This may not be a lasting measure, yet I found this a source of help for a clean and fresher breath.

The observance of these simple rules will not only ensure that you have a productive fast but also help you to deal with bad breath when fasting.

Luke 2:52

And Jesus increased in wisdom and stature, and in favour with God and man.

CHAPTER FIVE

What to do when you are fasting

Your fasting is more than just physical bodily exercise. If this is true, then there are some spiritual protocol that you have to follow for your fasting to make an impact.

Often, believers are fasting but see little or no result from their fast. The reason for this abound in failing to take action that is required of a venture like fasting. Jesus had to caution that we should not fast like the hypocrites. By breaking spiritual rules, we make our fasting and prayer useless and the activity will not be different from the worldly men and women who abstain from food for purely fashionable appearance –

weight loss. Our fasting must not be in that manner and fashion. We must do certain spiritual things that will make our fasting and prayer potent.

Avoid Public show

Matt 6:16

> *Moreover when ye fast, be not, as the hypocrites, of a sad countenance: for they disfigure their faces, that they may appear unto men to fast. Verily I say unto you, They have their reward.*

Every act of fasting is rewarded by God. Each time you fast and pray, God will reward you for fasting and praying. The scripture under reference cautions us to avoid any form of public show that may make people know that you are fasting. It may be largely impossible for anybody to carry a bell and ring that I am fasting. It sounds ridiculous! When you announce to men by your actions that you are fasting, you have missed the reward that follows that spiritual exercise. God knows and looks at the actions and the hearts of men. If by your conduct, the essence of what you are doing is to show to men that you are fasting, then you have lost your reward.

When you are in the company of believers who perceived that you are fasting, you can't say no. I am not fasting! By knowledge, they have already known that you are fasting. You will be lying if you say you aren't. What God is against is a deliberate and conscious effort to show people that you are fasting. If by chance, they get to know that you are fasting without any effort on your part to make them know that you are, then you will never lose your reward. If they are telling you because they know that you are fasting, you can be kind enough to tell them that you are waiting on the Lord, or you can tell them that you are on the mountain. The key that the Lord is watching is your heart. Are you making concerted effort to announce to people that you are fasting? Are you trying to let people know that you know how to fast? If you are, then I can tell you that you've lost your reward. No blessing is attached to such exercise.

When if fasting is for show or to prove a point, your physical human body may be enriched by your fasting, you gain no blessing and before God, it is a colossal waste of time.

The Bible tells us to anoint ourselves with oil so that we don't appear unto men to fast. Your countenance during the period of your fast is important.

The Word

The word of the Lord is a spiritual injection that you will need to subject your spirit man to whenever you are fasting. When fasting, your spirit man is open and can access spiritual signals. It means by implication that you can easily access information from the realm of the spirit. You may need to laden your spirit man with the word. Don't just fast alone, but combine this spiritual exercise with word intake. Put yourself on a steady diet of the word of God when fasting.

You have to subject yourself to a certain level of bible study.

There are certain times that you may be fasting, and you are working at a place where your job will give you all the needed time to study the Bible as you should. In some places, you will be so busy that you don't even have the time to look at the word. Praise God for our time and modern generation. Technology has permeated every aspect of our lives. You can have audio bible play in your ears while you work on your job. Never fast without downloading the word of God.

Job 23:12

> **Neither have I gone back from the commandment of his lips; I have esteemed the words of his mouth more than my necessary food.**

Job was saying that I value the word of his mouth more than my necessary food. The scripture is apt for the fasting period. If you value his word more than necessary food, then you would love to open it. And the word of God is the Bible, the written word. Fill your spirit man with the word of God as you fast. Combining the word, prayer and fasting together makes your fast potent.

Spiritual Materials

If you have gone on a long fast, you will see how gradually your strength wanes. For those who fast on water for days or certain fruits, you begin to feel some weakness. It may get to a point that taking steps may be difficult. If you can't pray at that point, you need to create a spiritual atmosphere and swim right inside it. You can get tapes, videos, messages, preaching and play them on your DVD player. The atmosphere will be charged and your fasting made productive. You can read spiritual books during this moment. The books will open your spirit man.

Talk less

When you are fasting ensure that you don't talk too much. Talking too much is like letting loose a spiritual tap. As you talk excessively, you are losing spiritual power. Your fasting becomes spiritually impactful when you do it in purity. The Bible makes us understand that talking too much can lead to sin and when you sin, the impact of your fast can't be effective. Talking too much leads to sin and iniquity. In the multitude of words, there is a sin. Talk when it is necessary to eliminate the chances of committing sin.

Proverbs 10:19

In the multitude of words there wanteth not sin: but he that refraineth his lips is wise.

Proverbs 4:7

Wisdom is the principal thing; therefore get wisdom: and with all thy getting get understanding.

CHAPTER SIX

Breaking Your Fast

Your fasting does not change God it changes you. It is an aid to your spiritual life. Your fasting does not change God's opinion about you. You are who you are before the eyes of the Lord. What your fasting does to you is to increase your spiritual fire. As you fast more and more, you are able to reach certain spiritual dimensions. You don't have to push your body beyond the limits because you are fasting. Wisdom is profitable to direct. The Bible says in all your getting get wisdom. It is with wisdom that the house is built. Whether you fast or not, I need to make this very clear that God has already promised to do what he says he would do. If you can stand on the word of God, the promises of God for your life will surely come to pass.

This wisdom nugget is good for your spiritual life so that you don't fast without wisdom. Towards this end, when you are fasting and you feel that your body cannot take it any longer, do not feign strength. There are several believers who have fasted to death. This certainly isn't the will of God for their lives. But you must always remember that we live in the body; the body is the horse that God has given unto us to do his will on the face of the earth. Some people just keep fasting even though the body is showing them several warning signals. They have forgotten that fasting requires wisdom.

There are certain sicknesses that will require you to see a doctor before you begin to fast. After consulting with your physician, and your body seems to protest when you fast, perform fasting that will not cause further problems to your health. Consult a physician if you are suffering from an ulcer that is in its advanced stage. Your physician will guide you or tell you what you are supposed to do. To begin a long fast when you are aware of the state of your body is to fast without wisdom. I have heard of brethren who fasted for 14 days, I mean a dry fast. After breaking their fast, they were all rushed to the hospital and they later died. When you hear things like this, sometimes you can begin to question God. Why should this have happened to the believers who were fasting? Well, I will say that believers fasted without wisdom.

You are not a spirit being. You're a human being with a spirit. You need to take care of your physical body so that you can use it to serve God very well. I am not trying to scare you. Even though I wrote this book out of the inspiration of the Holy Ghost, I have to tell you the truth when it comes to fasting. Friends, if you are on medication ensure you talk to your physician about the possibility of fasting.

For breastfeeding mum, prolong fast is discouraged during breastfeeding. This precautionary measure is necessary for those mums, who're carrying out exclusive breastfeeding for their children. At this stage, your baby depends on the food you eat for survival. The better you feed, the better nutritional food your baby is able to get when he sucks. Your baby draws liquid from your body. As a result of these, if you undertake a long fast, you can easily feel dizzy and tired. Fasting for a long period of time when you are breastfeeding can deprive your baby of essential nutrients from your body. Even if you are not carrying out exclusive breastfeeding, prolonged fasting is discouraged. For those who are not doing exclusive breastfeeding, there is still a need to consult their physician. To insist on fasting when on exclusive breastfeeding is to expose you and your baby to health dangers.

With the guidance of a physician, you can fast from morning until 12 PM. Every time you fast as a breastfeeding mother under the guidance of your physician, pay close attention to your physical body. If you experience severe discomfort, immediately discontinue the fast. You can continue fasting when your baby is weaned.

I need to balance this up. So that some people do not think that I am paying unnecessary attention to the flesh. What I am trying to say here is to guide you by telling you some simple wisdom tips that will help you when you fast.

Opening Your Fast

After praying and fasting for a while, especially if your fasting for a long period of time, a time will come that you may need to break your fast. During the period of a long fast, your intestine and body organs shrink due to the lack of eating food. Your entire body would be in dire need of nutrients. The food that you feed your body with after a long fast is important if the fasting you did was dry fasting.

First, you may need to drink warm water since you haven't eaten for a long period of time. After taking warm water for 30 minutes, then you can eat fruits. Solid food such as rice should never be used to break a long dry fast.

Romans 8:2

*For the law of the Spirit of
life in Christ Jesus hath
made me free from the law
of sin and death.*

CHAPTER SEVEN

Is There A Hard Rule For Fasting?

In general terms, there are no hard and fast rules concerning fasting. The Holy Spirit living inside of you is your number one partner when it comes to fasting. Don't be bound by ironclad rules. Fasting normally affects the body. When it is carried on for a long time, the effect is felt on the knees, joint, and general tiredness. This is due to the absence of solid food in the body or it may be caused by the absence of liquid in the body. As such, tiredness will be felt in these parts of the body.

Do not be bound by a time when you fast. You are not fasting under the law watching out the time to ensure that you hit a particular spot on the clock. If you do that, you are behaving like time watchers.

If you experience weakness in the body, don't feel guilty about taking water. You are not fasting to prove a point. You are equally not fasting to show people how much you can fast. What you are doing is a spiritual exercise that will fetch you an eternal reward. So approach your fast with the different mindset. God is the one watching you not man.

Even when you drink water don't feel guilty about it. As a matter of fact, there are many times I had to drink water when I am fasting. I didn't feel guilty about it because I was not competing with anyone. Neither was I fasting to show anything to anybody. My fast was done to the Lord the one who sees in secret and rewards men openly.

A fast is productive when it is done under the leading of the Holy Ghost. So when you are fasting and the Holy Ghost says drink some water obey that instruction without hesitation. Don't disobey the instruction because you wanted to reach a certain time of the day before eating.

The believer's closest companion when it comes to fasting and prayer is the Holy Ghost. He is the one that supplies the grace and power to fast and pray. Without the Holy Ghost, fasting will be very difficult to embark upon. Therefore, do not be bound by rules to the extent that you disobey the instructions of the Holy Ghost when you are fasting. The essence of Christianity now is to be led by the spirit of God. It is the leading of the Holy Ghost that confirms whether you belong to God or not. Don't rely on rules so much that you disregard the counsel of the Holy Spirit.

Luke 18:1

And he spake a parable unto them to this end, that men ought always to pray, and not to faint;

CHAPTER EIGHT

How to Pray When You Are Fasting

To get the best out of your fasting and prayer, there is a particular way to pray. A long fast will certainly bear on your body and strength will rapidly decline as the days travel by. So there is a need to pray to God for strength and power whenever you fast and pray.

Pray scripture-based prayers. Before the commencement of your fast, search your Bible and find Scriptures that tackled the areas of your need that prompted the fasting and prayer. Write down the Scriptures and used them to pray while you are fasting.

Begin each prayer point by reading the Scripture and then pray about it. Scripture-based prayer is very potent if the right approach is used.

Where you are unable to get specific Scriptures that address the concerns which led to your fast, then use general Scriptures. For instance, Philippians 4:19 says God will supply all of your needs according to his riches in glory. So if you are praying for divine supplies; you couldn't find a particular Scripture that suits what you are praying for, then you can rely on the book of Philippians chapter four verse 19 which covers everything on divine supplies. General Scriptures are good when the believer is unable to find specific Scriptures that cover the area of his need.

Friends, never begin your fast without stockpiling Scriptures to be used for your prayers. Use these Scriptures when knocking on heavens doors. I believe that you will receive your answers without delay.

Prayers Before Fasting

1 Samuel 2:9

He will keep the feet of his saints, and the wicked shall be silent in darkness; for by strength shall no man prevail.

Zachariah 4:6

Then he answered and spake unto me, saying, This is the word of the Lord unto Zerubbabel, saying, Not by might, nor by power, but by my spirit, saith the Lord of hosts.

Philippians 1:6

Being confident of this very thing, that he which hath begun a good work in you will perform it until the day of Jesus Christ:

Father, I make demands for supernatural strength and empowerment as I begin my fasting and prayers in the name of Jesus. I asked that you quicken every part of my body and my spirit man to fast as I should in the name of Jesus.

Father in the name of Jesus, I ask for the grace to pray and fast in this season in the mighty name of Jesus. Strengthen my spirit man to be able to pray as I ought to in the name of Jesus. I know that the power of the flesh may fail me, but the spirit can empower me to pray.

Thank you, Lord, for the privilege to fast and pray. I know that by your word you are a God that always complete whatever you start. Therefore, I pray for the finishers grace in the mighty name of Jesus. This fast that I have started today, I will do it until I finish it in the name of Jesus. Amen.

Prayers of Spiritual Sensitivity

Romans 8:14

For as many as are led by the Spirit of God, they are the sons of God.

Isaiah 30:21

And thine ears shall hear a word behind thee, saying, This is the way, walk ye in it, when ye turn to the right hand, and when ye turn to the left.

Father in the mighty name of Jesus, I make demands for the grace to be spiritually sensitive to your spirit. I ask that you give me the grace to be able to hear every form of spiritual instruction that would come forth at this season of my fast.

Father in the name of Jesus, I pray for the grace to obey all spiritual instruction that may come from the Holy Spirit, in this season in the mighty name of Jesus.

Prayer against the Spirit of Distraction

1 Corinthians 7:35

And this I speak for your own profit; not that I may cast a snare upon you, but for that which is comely, <u>and that ye may attend upon the Lord</u>

**_without   distraction_.
(Underlining mine)**

Father in the mighty name of Jesus, I pray against every spirit of distraction that may hinder me from picking up spiritual signals during the period of my prayer and fasting in the mighty name of Jesus. I take authority over every form of spiritual distraction in this season in the mighty name of Jesus.

Prayers in the Midst of Your Fasting

Isaiah 58:6

> **_Is not this the fast that I have chosen? to loose the bands of wickedness, to undo the heavy burdens, and to let the oppressed go free, and that ye break every yoke?_**

Father today, by the authority in the name of Jesus, I break every heavy burden upon my life in the name of Jesus. By the power of this prayer and fasting that I am doing, I decree my freedom in the name of Jesus. Amen

Prayers of Appreciation for the privilege to fast

Philippians 2:13

For it is God which worketh in you both to will and to do of his good pleasure.

Psalms 136:3

O give thanks to the Lord of lords: for his mercy endureth for ever.

Psalms 124:1-4

1 If it had not been the Lord who was on our side, now may Israel say;
2 If it had not been the Lord who was on our side, when men rose up against us:
3 Then they had swallowed us up quick, when their wrath was kindled against us:
4 Then the waters had overwhelmed us, the stream had gone over our soul:

1 John 5:14-15

> **14 And this is the confidence that we have in him, that, if we ask any thing according to his will, he heareth us:**
> **15 And if we know that he hear us, whatsoever we ask, we know that we have the petitions that we desired of him.**

Father in the mighty name of Jesus, I appreciate you for the grace and strength supplied to me throughout the period of my fasting in the name of Jesus. Thank you for empowering me to you be all the glory and to you be all the honour in the name of Jesus.

Father, I want to praise you for all you have done for me as I fasted. It was only because of you that this fasting was not overwhelming on my body. You stood by me and gave me strength all the way to the conclusion of this fast. I want to thank you for all you've done because I know that I couldn't have achieved these with my strength. So, father, I have come here to return all the glory to your name for what you have done for me in the name of Jesus, Amen.

Father in the mighty name of Jesus, thank you for answering all of my prayers during the period of this fast in Jesus name. I appreciate you because this is the confidence I having you whenever I come before you with any requests in prayer you always answer. Thank you, father, because my prayer request has been turned into testimonies and praise reports all to the glory of your name.

Father in the name of Jesus, I want to use this opportunity to especially thank you for your mercies that I have seen while I fasted. It was available in the measure I can't quantify. To you be all the glory and all the honour for this great thing that you have done in the name of Jesus. Amen.

Free E-book For You!!!

Download this e-book for free and receive our spiritual enhancing contents

https://bit.ly/2W4qgLK

Other books by the same Author

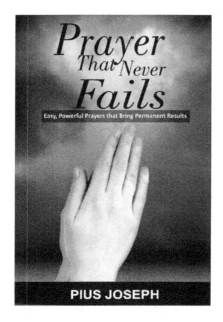

Prayer That Never Fails

VISION
FROM THE
HEAVENLY

PIUS
JOSEPH

Vision From The Heavenly - Kindle edition by Pius Joseph. Religion & Spirituality Kindle eBook

Check our blog: www.thetentofglory.com

Made in the USA
Monee, IL
28 April 2022